BERKLEE
INSTANT
GUITAR

TOMO FUJITA

Edited by
JONATHAN FEIST

Berklee Media
Associate Vice President: Dave Kusek
Director of Content: Debbie Cavalier
Marketing Manager: Jennifer Rassler

Berklee Press
Senior Writer/Editor: Jonathan Feist
Writer/Editor: Susan Gedutis
Production Manager: Shawn Girsberger
Contributing Illustrator: Louis Ochoa

ISBN 0-634-02951-7

DISTRIBUTED BY

1140 Boylston Street
Boston, MA 02215-3693 USA
(617) 747-2146

Visit Berklee Press Online at
www.berkleepress.com

HAL•LEONARD®
CORPORATION
7777 W. BLUEMOUND RD. P.O. BOX 13819
MILWAUKEE, WISCONSIN 53213

Visit Hal Leonard Online at
www.halleonard.com

For my children, Nathaniel, Samantha, and Michael.

Contents

CD Tracks

The Band

Tomo Fujita, *Guitar*
Larry Finn, *Drums*
Dave Limina, *Keyboard*
Jim Lamond, *Bass*

Basics

CD 1.   Tuning Note High E
CD 2.   Tuning Note B
CD 3.   Tuning Note G
CD 4.   Tuning Note D
CD 5.   Tuning Note A
CD 6.   Tuning Note Low E

Lesson 1. Playing a Note

CD 7.   Open E played and then muted
CD 8.   "High E Rock" Full Band
CD 9.   "High E Rock" Play Along

Lesson 2. Power Chords

CD 10.   E5 Power Chord
CD 11.   "Power Down" Full Band
CD 12.   "Power Down" Play Along

Lesson 3. Keeping Time

CD 13.   E5 Whole Notes
CD 14.   "Whole E Rock" Full Band
CD 15.   "Whole E Rock" Play Along
CD 16.   "Rock A-Round" Full Band
CD 17.   "Rock A-Round" Play Along
CD 18.   "Stadium" Full Band
CD 19.   "Stadium" Play Along

Lesson 4. Movable Chords

CD 20.   "Starting Out" Full Band
CD 21.   "Starting Out" Play Along
CD 22.   "Stepping Forward" Full Band
CD 23.   "Stepping Forward" Play Along
CD 24.   "Destination" Full Band
CD 25.   "Destination" Play Along

Lesson 5. Connecting the Dots

CD 26.   "Connected to You" Full Band
CD 27.   "Connected to You" Play Along

Lesson 6. Riffs

CD 28.   "Riffage" Full Band
CD 29.   "Riffage" Play Along
CD 30.   "Riffin' Up" Full Band
CD 31.   "Riffin' Up" Play Along
CD 32.   "Chuck's Riff" Full Band
CD 33.   "Chuck's Riff" Play Along
CD 34.   "Rotten Pick" Full Band
CD 35.   "Rotten Pick" Play Along
CD 36.   "Heavy Picking" Full Band
CD 37.   "Heavy Picking" Play Along

Lesson 7. Funk

CD 38.   "What the Funk" Full Band
CD 39.   "What the Funk" Play Along
CD 40.   "Funkified" Full Band
CD 41.   "Funkified" Play Along

Lesson 8. Open Chords

CD 42.   "Opener" Full Band
CD 43.   "Opener" Play Along
CD 44.   "Cashing In" Full Band
CD 45.   "Cashing In" Play Along
CD 46.   "Open Up" Full Band
CD 47.   "Open Up" Play Along
CD 48.   "Move It" Full Band
CD 49.   "Move It" Play Along

Lesson 9. Minor Chords

CD 50.   "Light to Dark" Full Band
CD 51.   "Light to Dark" Play Along
CD 52.   "Bittersweet" Full Band
CD 53.   "Bittersweet" Play Along

Lesson 10. Alternate Picking

Lesson 11. Barre Chords

Welcome to Instant Guitar

This book will get you playing the guitar instantly. Some friends and I put together a band, and we recorded some really fun music for you to jam on with us. The *Instant Guitar* CD has songs ready for you to play along with *right now*!

For each tune, first check out CD tracks marked "Listen," which have me playing guitar. Then, once you've learned the guitar parts, it's your turn. Tracks marked "Play" have no guitar part.

So, get your guitar out of the case, and let's play some music!

Basics

The Guitar

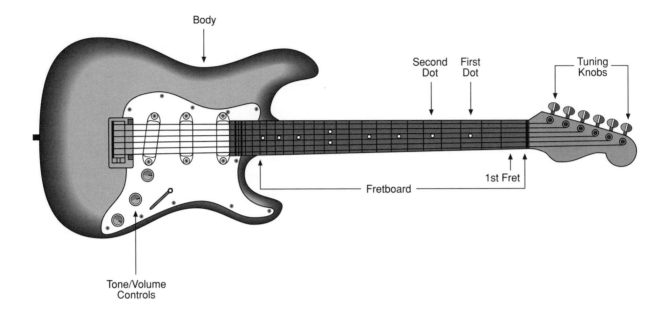

Other equipment needed: guitar amplifier, 1/4" cable, CD player.

Plugging In

1. With the amplifier off, set all knobs to the twelve o'clock position. Set the master volume to zero.

2. Plug the cable into your guitar. Plug the other end into the amp's input.

3. Turn on the amp.

4. Turn the guitar's volume knob up all the way, and pluck a string. You should not hear anything.

5. Slowly turn up the amp's master volume. Pluck a string. Find an amp volume setting that lets you hear your guitar comfortably.

6. You can always lower the volume on your guitar once the amp is set up.

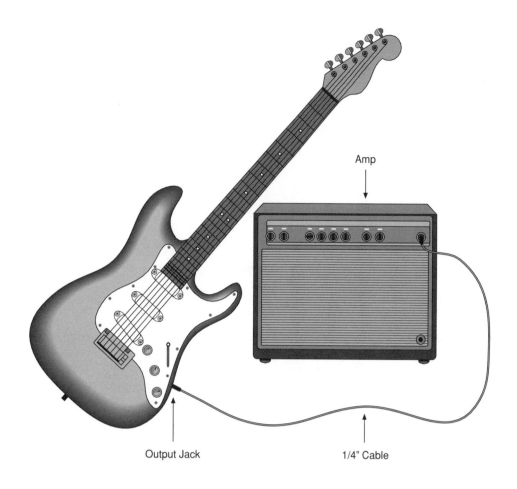

Amp

Output Jack

1/4" Cable

Strings

The guitar has six strings—from lowest sounding to highest sounding: E, A, D, G, B, E. The strings are shown as they appear when you look down at the guitar, while you are in playing position.

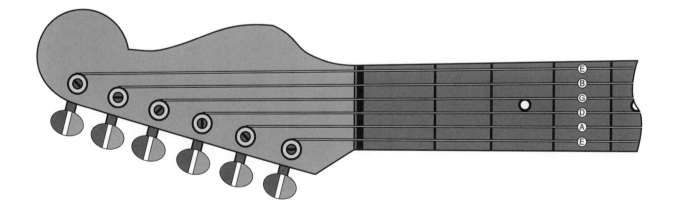

Tuning

There are lots of ways to tune. Here's how to do it with the CD.

 Tuning Note High E

1. Listen to CD track 1. Play the high open E string on your guitar.

2. To make these two E notes the same, determine whether the pitch of your E string is above or below the tuned pitch on the CD.

3. While the E string sounds, turn its tuning knob until the string is at the same pitch as the CD's tuning note.

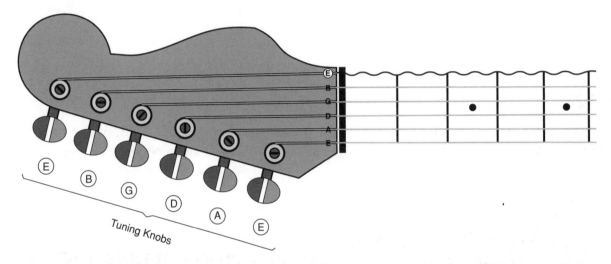

If your string sounds lower than the CD (flat), it is too loose, so tighten the tuning knob. If your string sounds higher than the CD (sharp), it is too tight, so loosen the tuning knob.

Try to hear the "beats," as your guitar note gets closer to being in tune. When your string is tuned, the beats will stop.

Tune your other five strings in the same way, and you're ready to play!

2 **Tuning Note B**

3 **Tuning Note G**

4 **Tuning Note D**

5 **Tuning Note A**

6 **Tuning Note Low E**

Playing a Note

The high open E is the highest and smallest string.

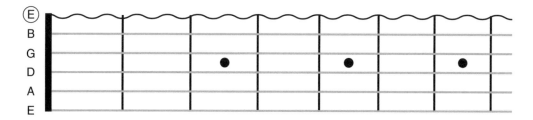

7 Listen

Listen to the sound of a high open E, and then play it yourself. Pluck the string downward with the pick, holding it as shown.

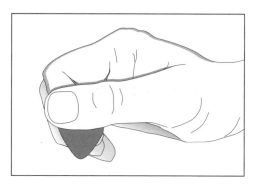

Muting

To mute (silence) the strings, touch them with your left hand.

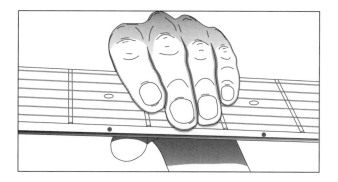

Play

Play a high open E and then mute it. You may hear a ringing in the other strings when you play. Touch them to mute this ringing.

"High E Rock"

This first tune, "High E Rock," is played on the high open E string.

 1. Listen

If you can play the high open E, you can play this tune. Listen to the guitar on the CD. That's the only note played.

9 2. Play

Now, play "High E Rock" with the band on the CD. Follow your ear. Play long notes, short notes, loud or soft notes—just play the high E and ROCK!

Congratulations, you just played your first rock tune!

Power Chords

E5 Power Chord

A *power chord* is two notes: a root and its fifth. Listen to the CD and notice the two different notes. Here's the notation for the E5 power chord.

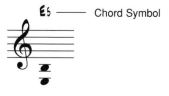

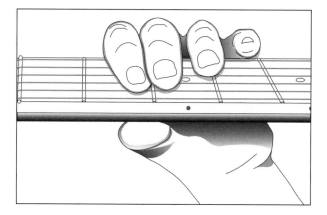

The *root* (low note) of E5 is the note E. It is the lowest string on your guitar.

Listen to just the open E and then the E5 power chord. Then, pluck the low E string, moving your pick downward. At the end of your stroke, your pick should rest on the A string.

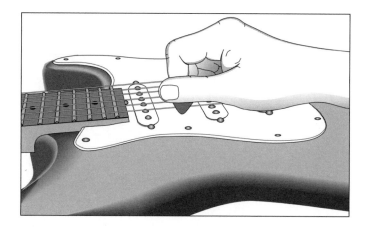

Fretted Notes

To change a string's note, press the string all the way down on the fingerboard between any two fret bars.

The other note of E5 is B, also called its *fifth*. This is a fretted note on the A string. Hold down the A string with your index finger at the second fret. Play both the E and the B together. The two notes should sound at the same time. Listen again to track 10 to make sure you are playing the same notes.

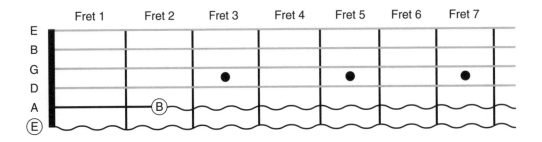

Tablature

Tablature (or just "tab") shows a note's fret number. Tab has six lines, showing the six strings. On the lines are numbers, showing what fret you should press to get the note.

Here is E5 with its tablature. The 0 on the E string means an open note, and the 2 on the A string means to hold down that string at the second fret. It looks like the fretboard diagrams you have been reading.

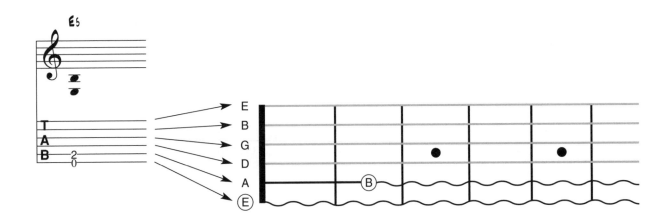

Strum downwards, from the low E string through the A string. This is called a *down stroke*. Sound both the strings at once. At the end of the stroke, your pick should rest on the D string.

"Power Down"

The next tune, "Power Down," is played with an E5 power chord.

 ## 1. Listen

If you can play E5, you can play this tune. Listen to the guitar on the CD. That's the only chord played.

 ## 2. Play

Now, play "Power Down" with the band on the CD. As in "High E Rock," follow your ear, and play what sounds good. Just play E5 and ROCK!

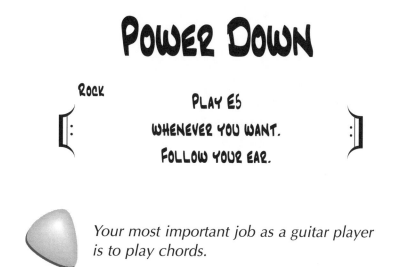

Your most important job as a guitar player is to play chords.

Keeping Time

Whole Notes

This is an E5 whole note (**o**). It lasts four beats. Count "1 2 3 4."

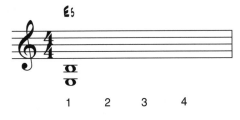

13 Listen to the bass drum. It plays four beats while the guitar holds each E5 whole note. The guitar plays with the drums on beat 1 of every bar. Count along as you listen.

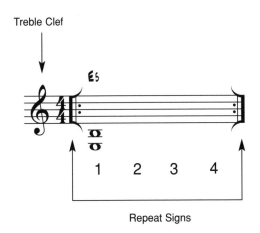

> ***Tip:*** *When you see these signs* [: :] *, repeat the music between them.*

"Whole E Rock"

14 ### 1. Listen

This tune is like "Power Down," but the guitar plays steady whole notes.

15 ### 2. Play

Play along with "Whole E Rock." Hook up with bass drum on beat 1 of every bar.

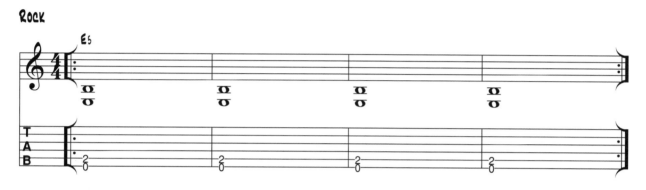

> **Tip:** Play at **exactly** the same time as the bass drum on beat 1. This is called **hooking up** with the drummer.

A5 Power Chord

The A5 power chord is like E5 except that it is on the A and D strings.

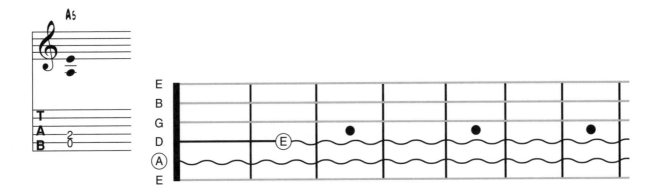

"Rock A-Round"

 1. Listen

This guitar part is like the one in "Whole E Rock," but it is played on the A and D strings.

 2. Play

Hook up with the bass drum on beat 1. Let your A5 power chord ring for beats 2, 3, and 4.

ROCK A-ROUND

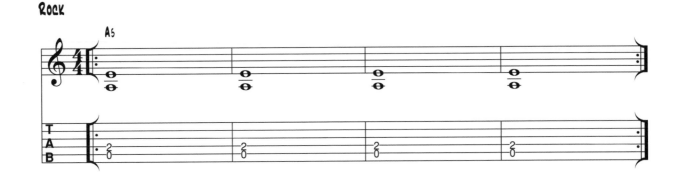

"Stadium"

 1. Listen

This guitar part to "Stadium" combines the E5 and A5 power chords.

 2. Play

Make sure to mute your strings before playing the next note.

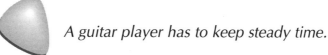

A guitar player has to keep steady time.

Movable Chords

First Dot: G5

Play E5, but this time, hold down the B (A string, second fret) with your *ring finger*.

We will use this same hand position to play power chord G5. Slide your ring finger down the fingerboard, and hold down the A string at the second dot (fifth fret). Hold down the E string with your index finger at the first dot (third fret).

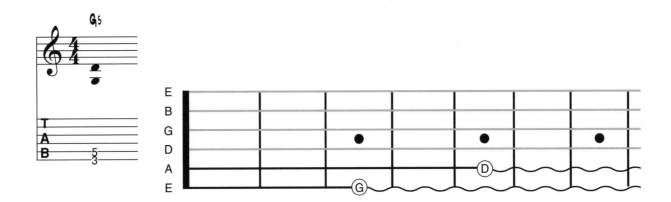

Holding down these two strings, play the G5 power chord.

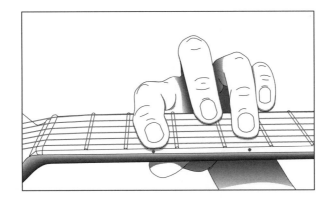

"Starting Out"

 1. Listen

Count along while you listen, "1 2 3 4, 1 2 3 4, ..."

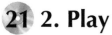 **2. Play**

Play an E5 whole note. Then play a G5 whole note. That's all you need to play this tune.

First Dot: C5

The next tune is the same thing, but moved to the A and D strings. Play A5, but with your ring finger on the D string. Then, to play the C5 power chord, play the note C on the A string at the first dot (third fret), holding down the string with your left index finger. Play its fifth, G, on the D string by holding down your ring finger at the second dot (fifth fret). Strum both together as the C5 power chord.

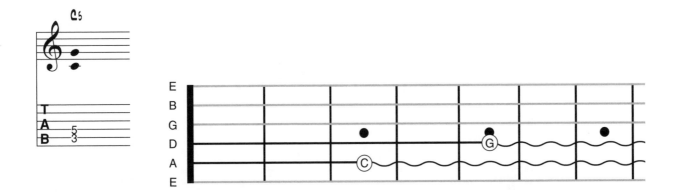

"Stepping Forward"

22 **1. Listen**

Count along while you listen, "1 2 3 4, 1 2 3 4 . . ."

23 **2. Play**

Play an A5 power chord. Then play a C5 power chord. That's all you need to play "Stepping Forward."

STEPPING FORWARD

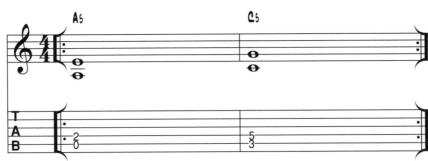

Movable Chords

The four power chords you have been playing are similar. Play them all, one after the other. Notice that they share a shape: from the root, the fifth is on the next string, down two frets.

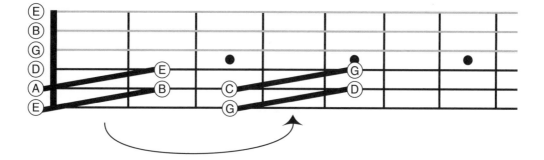

This shape will give you a power chord up and down the fingerboard. That is why it is called a *movable* chord shape: you can "move" it around the fingerboard. When you want to play a power chord, just remember this chord shape: over one string, down two frets. Your fingers stay in the same position.

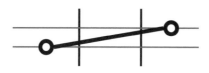

"Destination"

24 1. Listen

"Destination" combines the power chords in "Starting Out" and "Stepping Forward."

25 2. Play

As you play, think about the power chord shape.

DESTINATION

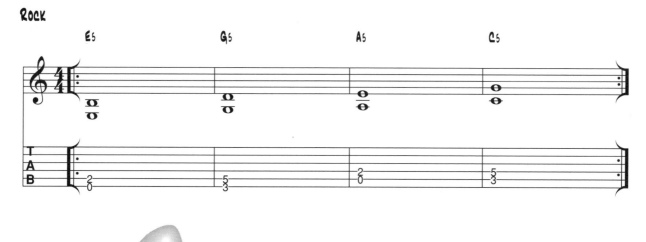

Chord shapes make learning chords much easier.

Connecting the Dots

Second Dot: A5 and D5

You will use the power chord shape to help you find these chords.

Find the note A, but this time, play it on the second dot of the E string (fifth fret). Using the power chord shape, build the A5 chord, playing the E on the A string, third dot (seventh fret).

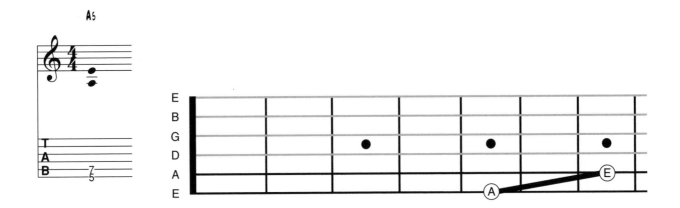

Find D5, building its root from the second dot of the A string (fifth fret).

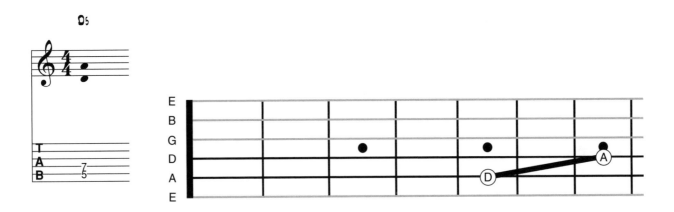

The next tune, "Connected to You," combines power chords built from roots at the first and second dots. These roots form another shape: a box. This shape will help you learn the tune.

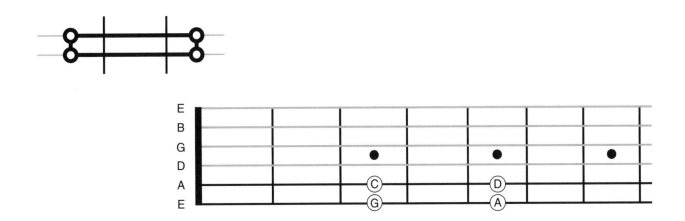

"Connected to You"

 26 **1. Listen**

Follow the music as you listen to this tune. The guitar plays *half notes*. Half notes ($\textstyle\int$) get two beats.

> **Tip:** Count along with the beat, "1 2 3 4." This will help you hook up with the rest of the band, and get you inside the song's rhythm.

27 **2. Play**

Remember the chord shape as you play.

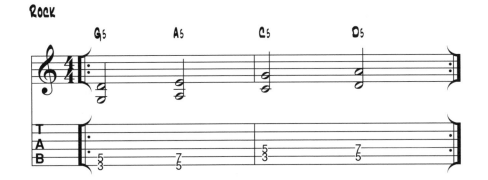

> **Tip:** Remembering shapes is easier than remembering notes. Look for shapes whenever you learn any music.

Riffs

Riffs are repeated patterns of notes. They are often the most memorable part of a rock song. This next guitar part is a riff. First, play the E5 power chord, with your index finger on the second fret. Then, change the B to a C♯ by using your ring finger up two frets on the A string.

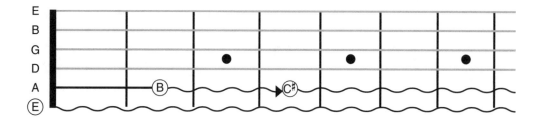

"Riffage"

28 ## 1. Listen

Follow the music as you listen to this tune. The guitar plays *quarter notes*. Quarter notes (♩) get one beat.

29 ## 2. Play

Press the string very softly. When you press at the fourth fret with your ring finger, keep your index finger down on the second fret. Don't move your ring finger too far away from the string!

Moving the Pattern

This riff is the same pattern used in "Riffage," but it is on the A and D strings.

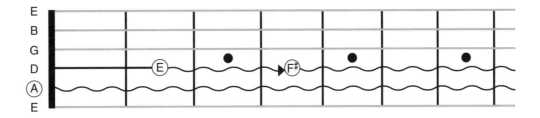

"Riffin' Up"

 ### 1. Listen

Listen to the steady quarter notes.

 ### 2. Play

Be careful not to pick the E string, playing only on the A and D strings. You can try muting the E string with your right-hand palm.

"Chuck's Riff"

32 ## 1. Listen

This tune uses the rock blues riffs you have been playing.

33 ## 2. Play

To play "Chuck's Riff," first play the riff from "Riffage." Then play the riff from "Riffin' Up." Keep repeating this eight-bar pattern.

Chuck's Riff

Rock Blues

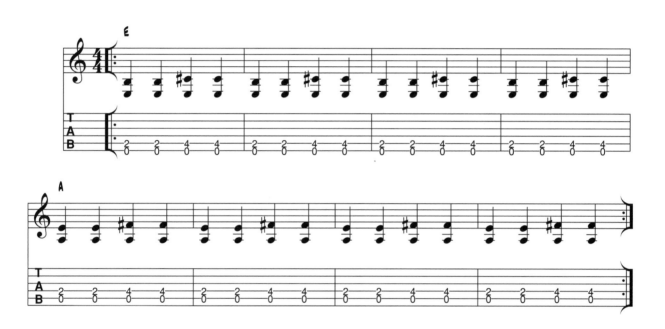

> ### *On the Scene*
> *Guitar pioneer Chuck Berry used this riff as the foundation for many songs.*

Heavy Rock Picking Pattern

Heavy rock, punk, and some other styles that have heavy power-chord riffs are often played with all down strokes. The music may be marked with a (⊓).

These styles often have an eighth-note feel. *Eighth notes* (♪♪♪♪) are twice as fast as quarter notes (♩ ♩). There are two eighth notes in one beat.

"Rotten Pick"

 ### 1. Listen

Listen to the steady eighth notes in the drums and bass.

 ### 2. Play

Play these chords on the E and A string. Use all down strokes. Remember the shape for power chords.

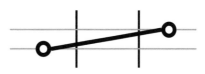

ROTTEN PICK

"Heavy Picking"

36 ## 1. Listen

Listen carefully to where the chords change.

37 ## 2. Play

This tune brings back the power chord C5. Play the root C on the A string, first dot (third fret).

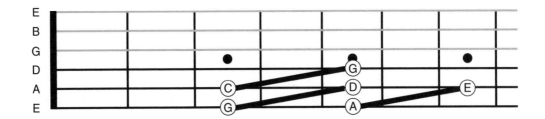

> **Tip:** *Thinking about two shapes will help you play this tune. First, remember the power chord shape.*
>
>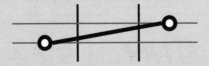
>
> *Second, remember the shape that the bottom notes move in for this tune.*
>
>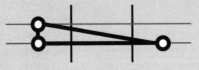

HEAVY PICKING

HARD ROCK

Shapes make it easier to play around the entire fingerboard.

Funk

Funk music has very strong bass and drum parts. Listen to these instruments when you play the next several tunes.

 ## "What the Funk"

1. Listen

A *quarter rest* (𝄽) means "don't play for one beat." Hook up with the bass drum on this rhythm. Listen for the snare drum when you rest on beats 2 and 4.

 ### 2. Play

Use all down strokes for these power chords.

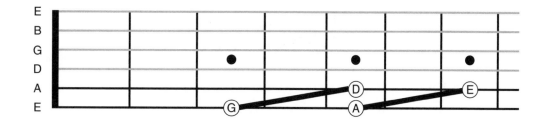

WHAT THE FUNK

"Funkified"

40 ## 1. Listen

This tune also has the funk rhythm. There is a new power chord, but the part is just like "What the Funk," but played on the A and D strings.

41 ## 2. Play

Hook up with the bass and drums.

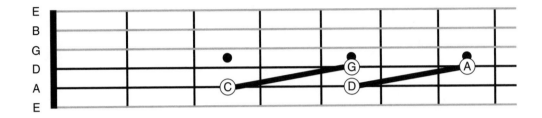

Open Chords

Open chords include some of the guitar's open strings.

Open E Chord

To strum an open E major chord, finger three notes. The other notes are played on open strings. Notice that the bottom two notes are the E power chord.

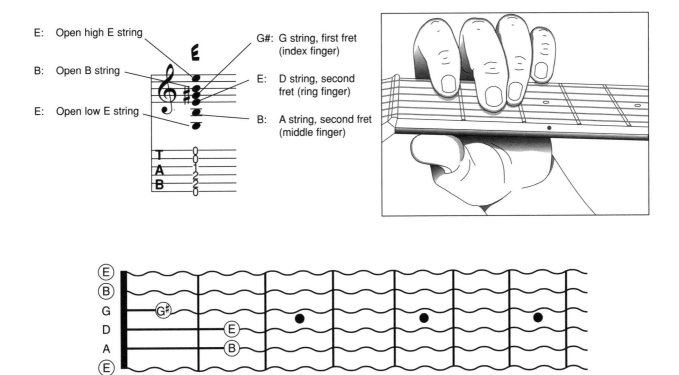

E: Open high E string
B: Open B string
E: Open low E string

G#: G string, first fret (index finger)
E: D string, second fret (ring finger)
B: A string, second fret (middle finger)

Strum a down stroke from the low E string through the high E string. Sound all the strings at once.

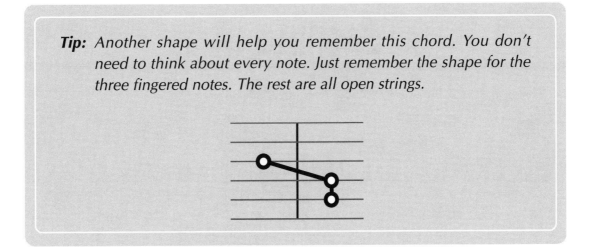

> **Tip:** *Another shape will help you remember this chord. You don't need to think about every note. Just remember the shape for the three fingered notes. The rest are all open strings.*

"Opener"

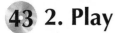 **1. Listen**

The guitar part to this tune is all quarter notes.

2. Play

Play steady quarter-note open E chords. Use all downstrokes.

OPENER

POP ROCK

"Cashing In"

44 1. Listen

This tune also uses an open E chord. Rather than playing all notes at once, the two low notes (E and B) alternate with the top part of the chord.

45 2. Play

Your left hand stays in the same position. Your right hand plays the correct strings.

CASHING IN

COUNTRY

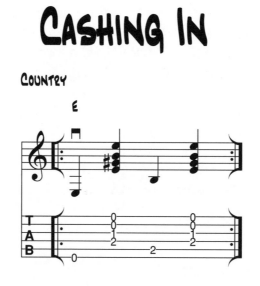

24

Open A Chord

The open A major chord also has three fingered notes, and they are all fingered on the second fret. The other strings are open. Strum this chord beginning on the A string, leaving the E string unplayed.

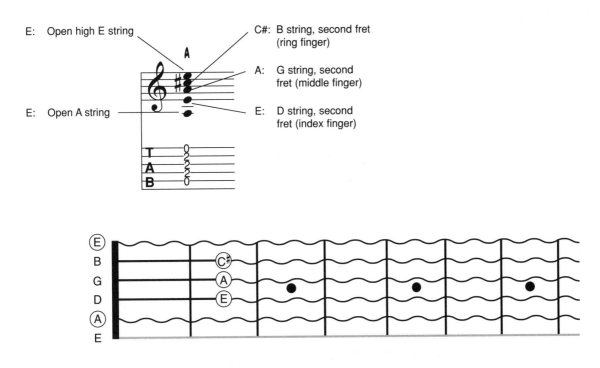

E: Open high E string

E: Open A string

C#: B string, second fret (ring finger)

A: G string, second fret (middle finger)

E: D string, second fret (index finger)

This shape will help you remember the open A chord.

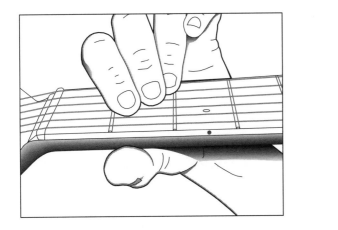

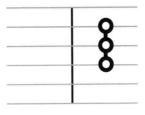

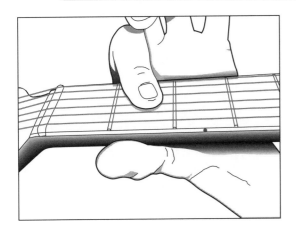

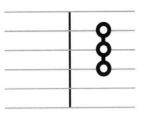

Tip: You could also play all three fingered notes with your index finger. Use which ever way is more comfortable.

"Open Up"

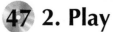

46 1. Listen

This tune uses an open A chord.

47 2. Play

Play from the fifth to the first string.

POP ROCK

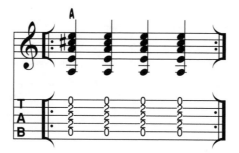

26

"Move It"

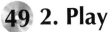 **1. Listen**

This tune uses the two open chords you have been playing.

49 2. Play

Before you play, practice moving from one chord to the other.

MOVE IT

COUNTRY ROCK

Tip: *Thinking about the shapes will simplify changing between these two chords. Notice their similarities. Two neighboring strings are played at the same fret.*

Minor Chords

Minor chords have a different sound than major chords.

Open E Minor Chord

The open E minor chord (E–) is similar to the E major chord (E) shown in lesson 8, except that it has only two fingered notes, not three. First play E major.

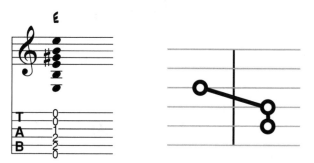

Then, lift your index finger from the G string, and play E minor.

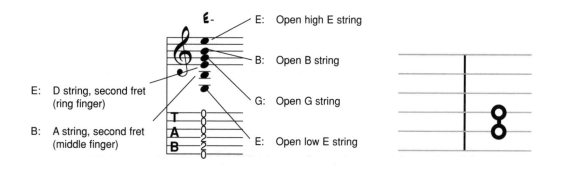

E: D string, second fret (ring finger)

B: A string, second fret (middle finger)

E: Open high E string

B: Open B string

G: Open G string

E: Open low E string

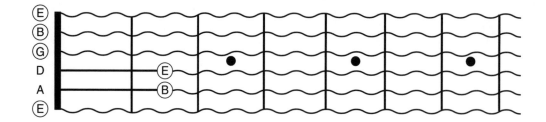

"Light to Dark"

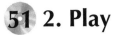 ### 1. Listen

This tune uses the E minor and major chords.

 ### 2. Play

Before you play, practice moving from one chord to the other.

Open A Minor Chord

The open A minor chord (A–) is fingered similarly to the E major chord. All of your fingers move over one string, but the shape is the same. First, play E major.

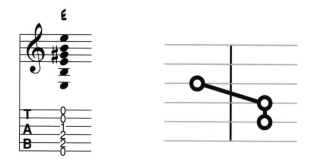

To play A minor, shift all three fingers one string higher (towards the high E string).

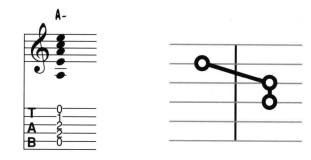

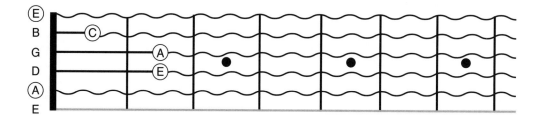

"Bittersweet"

 1. Listen

This tune uses four chords.

> *Tip:* A natural (♮) cancels out a sharp.

53 2. Play

Before you play, practice moving from one chord to the other.

BITTERSWEET

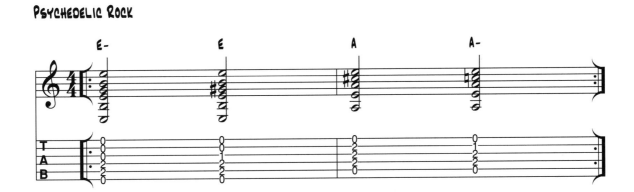

PSYCHEDELIC ROCK

Lesson 10 Alternate Picking

On some eighth-note grooves, you will want to use *alternate picking*. Instead of all down strokes, you "alternate" between down strokes (your hand strums downward) and *up strokes* (your hand strums upward). Up strokes are marked with a (⋁).

Alternate picking lets you play faster rhythms. It also has a more varied sound.

"Strumming"

54 1. Listen

Listen to the eighth-note rhythms.

> **Tip:** Sometimes, you will see slashes (♩) instead of dots for the noteheads. Read the chord symbol or tablature for what notes to play. The slashes show rhythm only.

55 2. Play

Play E minor chords in eighth notes.

FOLK ROCK

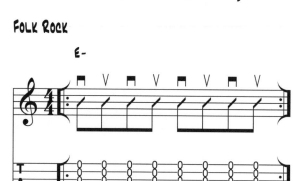

Open G Major Chord

Play the open G major chord. Memorize its chord shape.

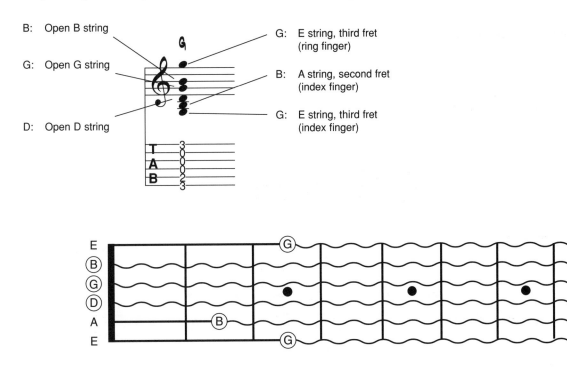

B: Open B string

G: Open G string

D: Open D string

G: E string, third fret (ring finger)

B: A string, second fret (index finger)

G: E string, third fret (index finger)

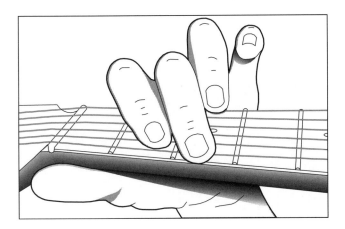

This shape will help you remember the open G major chord.

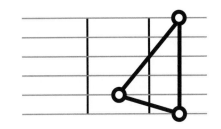

"E-Go Freak"

 1. Listen

This tune mixes quarter-note and eighth-note rhythms.

 **2. Play**

Be sure to use the down strokes and up strokes shown. Use your ear, and hook up with the recording.

Tip: Keep your picking hand in constant motion.

For an added challenge, learn the C and D open chords. Practice them, memorize their shapes, and then try the tune, "Touch the Moon."

C Open Chord

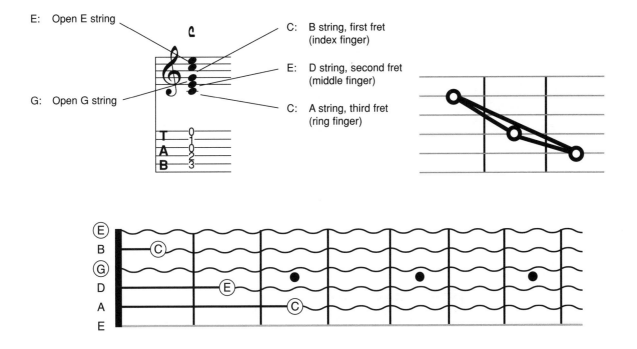

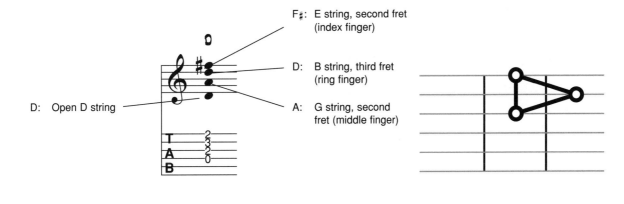

D Open chord

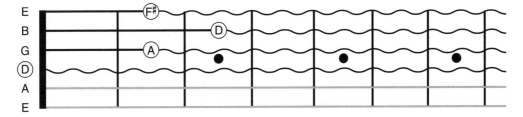

"Touch the Moon"

58 **1. Listen**

This tune uses a new rhythm. Use your ear to learn the strumming pattern.

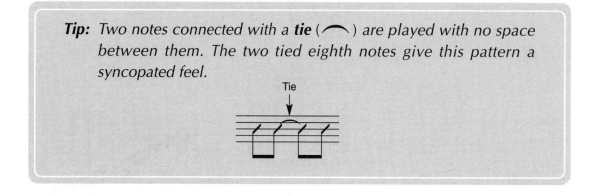

Tip: Two notes connected with a **tie** (⌒) are played with no space between them. The two tied eighth notes give this pattern a syncopated feel.

59 **2. Play**

Choose your own strumming pattern of down strokes and up strokes.

TOUCH THE MOON

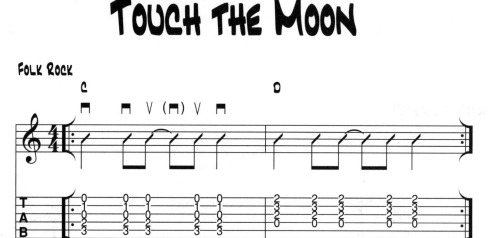

Barre Chords

Barre (pronounced "bar") chord shapes (or *forms*) are movable. They can get played on any fret. Learning one new barre-chord shape is like learning twelve new chords.

E Chord Form

Play an open E chord. Remember the shape?

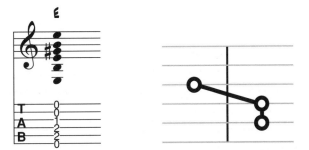

G Barre Chord

Now, we will play the G barre chord. With your left index finger, hold down *all six strings* at the first dot (third fret). Move the E chord's shape to frets 4 and 5, using the fingering shown.

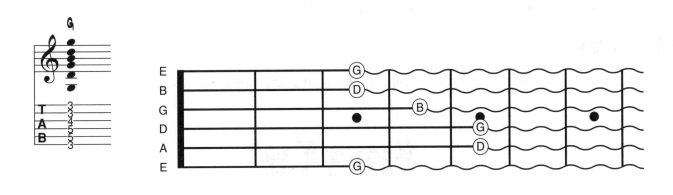

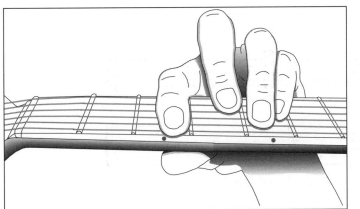

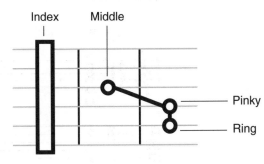

A Barre Chord

To play an A barre chord, move the shape to the second dot (fifth fret).

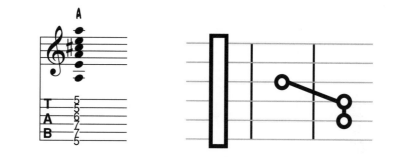

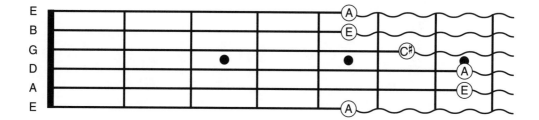

"Barre Tab"

60 ## 1. Listen

This tune uses the G and A barre chords you just learned.

61 ## 2. Play

Remember, the two chords are played using the same fingering moved up two frets.

BARRE TAB

Reggae/Ska

A Chord Form

First, play an open A chord. Remember the shape?

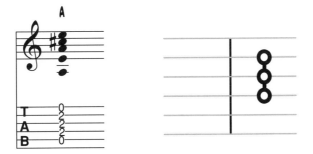

C Barre Chord

Now, we will play a C barre chord based on this shape. With your left index finger, hold down *all six strings* at the first dot (third fret). Move the A chord's shape to fret 5 (second dot). There are two ways to finger this. Try them both, and choose the one most comfortable for you.

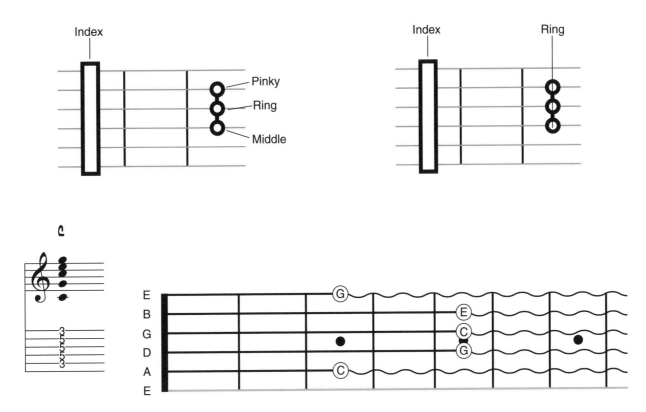

D Barre Chord

To play a D barre chord with this shape, move it to the second dot (fifth fret).

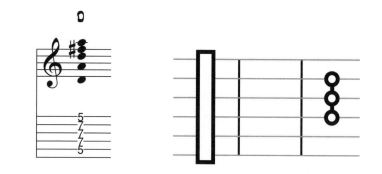

 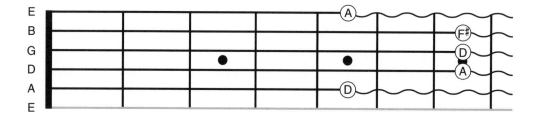

"Barre Hop"

62 ## 1. Listen

This tune uses the C and D barre chords you just learned.

63 ## 2. Play

Remember, the two chords are played using the same fingering moved up two frets.

BARRE HOP

Reggae/Ska

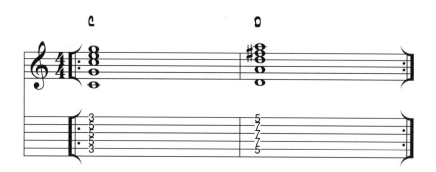

"Across the Barre"

 1. Listen

This tune combines the two barre-chord shapes you learned in this lesson.

 2. Play

Use the shapes to help you remember the chords.

"Instantaneous"

 1. Listen

This tune combines the barre-chord shapes you learned in this lesson.

 2. Play

The shapes will help you remember the chords.

INSTANTANEOUS

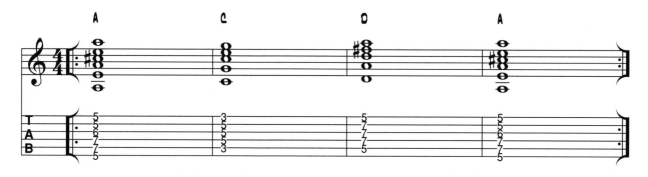

NICE SHOW!

Author's Note

Thanks for playing *Instant Guitar*. I hope you had fun playing these songs. The chords you've learned in this book are actually used in most of your favorite songs. Lots of music has the guitar playing chords and shapes just like the songs in this book.

Try playing along with any music and see if you can find where these chord forms fit in. Sometimes you have to move the shapes to different locations on the fingerboard to make the music sound good. Trial and error, and following your ear, eventually will lead you towards knowing where and when to use these chords, and others.

You have begun to hear how the guitar functions in music. Also, your hands are becoming comfortable with the fingerboard and the strings. Your guitar skills will get stronger the more you play.

I hope music and guitar playing enrich your life as they have mine.

—Tomo

Tomo Fujita uses: Combat Guitars, Ryo Guitars, Fender Amplifiers, D'Addario Strings, Pickboy Picks, Groove Tubes, and Celestion Speakers.

For more info, visit Tomo's Web site: http://www.tomofujita.com.

More Fine Publications from Berklee Press

As Serious About Music As You Are.

GUITAR

THE GUITARIST'S GUIDE TO COMPOSING AND IMPROVISING
▶ by Jon Damian
50449497 Book/CD..$24.95

BERKLEE BASIC GUITAR
▶ by William Leavitt
Phase 1
50449462 Book/Cassette $14.95
50449460 Book Only $7.95
Phase 2
50449470 Book Only $7.95

CLASSICAL STUDIES FOR PICK-STYLE GUITAR ▶ by William Leavitt
50449440 Book...$9.95

A MODERN METHOD FOR GUITAR 123 COMPLETE
▶ by William Leavitt
50449468 Book...$29.95
Also available in separate volumes:
Volume 1: Beginner
50449404 Book/CD...$22.95
50449400 Book Only $14.95
Volume 2: Intermediate
50449412 Book/Cassette $22.95
50449410 Book Only $14.95
Volume 3: Advanced
50449420 Book...$14.95

MELODIC RHYTHMS FOR GUITAR
▶ by William Leavitt
50449450 Book...$14.95

READING CONTEMPORARY GUITAR RHYTHMS ▶ by M. T. Szymczak
50449530 Book...$10.95

READING STUDIES FOR GUITAR
▶ by William Leavitt
50449490 Book...$14.95

ADVANCED READING STUDIES FOR GUITAR
▶ by William Leavitt
50449500 Book...$14.95

JIM KELLY GUITAR WORKSHOP SERIES

JIM KELLY'S GUITAR WORKSHOP
00695230 Book/CD...$14.95
00320144 Video/booklet $19.95
00320168 DVD/booklet $29.95

MORE GUITAR WORKSHOP
▶ by Jim Kelly
00695306 Book/CD...$14.95
00320158 Video/booklet $19.95

BASS

CHORD STUDIES FOR ELECTRIC BASS
▶ by Rich Appleman
50449750 Book...$14.95

INSTANT BASS ▶ by Danny Morris
50449502 Book/CD...$14.95

READING CONTEMPORARY ELECTRIC BASS
▶ by Rich Appleman
50449770 Book...$14.95

ROCK BASS LINES
▶ by Joe Santerre
50449478 Book/CD...$19.95

SLAP BASS LINES
▶ by Joe Santerre
50449508 Book/CD...$19.95

KEYBOARD

A MODERN METHOD FOR KEYBOARD
▶ by James Progris
50449620 Vol. 1: Beginner $14.95
50449630 Vol. 2: Intermediate $14.95
50449640 Vol. 3: Advanced $14.95

DRUM SET

BEYOND THE BACKBEAT
▶ by Larry Finn
50449447 Book/CD...$19.95

DRUM SET WARM-UPS
▶ by Rod Morgenstein
50449465 Book...$12.95

MASTERING THE ART OF BRUSHES
▶ by Jon Hazilla
50449459 Book/CD...$19.95

THE READING DRUMMER
▶ by Dave Vose
50449458 Book...$9.95

SAXOPHONE

CREATIVE READING STUDIES FOR SAXOPHONE ▶ by Joseph Viola
50449870 Book...$14.95

TECHNIQUE OF THE SAXOPHONE
▶ by Joseph Viola
50449820 Volume 1: Scale Studies $14.95
50449830 Volume 2: Chord Studies $14.95
50449840 Volume 3: Rhythm Studies $14.95

Berklee Press Publications feature material developed at the Berklee College of Music.
To browse the Berklee Press Catalog, go to www.berkleepress.com or visit your local music dealer or bookstore.

Prices subject to change without notice.

TOOLS FOR DJs

TURNTABLE TECHNIQUE: THE ART OF THE DJ
► by Stephen Webber
50449482 Book/2-Record Set $34.95

TURNTABLE BASICS ► by Stephen Webber
50449514 Book $9.95

VITAL VINYL, VOLUMES 1-5
► by Stephen Webber
12" records
50449491 Volume 1: Needle Juice $15.95
50449492 Volume 2: Turntablist's Toolkit........$15.95
50449493 Volume 3: Rockin' the House $15.95
50449494 Volume 4: Beat Bomb $15.95
50449495 Volume 5: Tech Tools for DJs $15.95

TOOLS FOR DJs SUPERPACK
► by Stephen Webber
50449529 Includes Turntable Technique book/2-record set and all 5 Vital Vinyl records (a $115 value!) ..$99.95

BERKLEE PRACTICE METHOD

Get Your Band Together

BASS ► by Rich Appleman and John Repucci
50449427 Book/CD $14.95

DRUM SET ► by Ron Savage and Casey Scheuerell
50449429 Book/CD $14.95

GUITAR ► by Larry Baione
50449426 Book/CD $14.95

KEYBOARD ► by Russell Hoffmann and Paul Schmeling
50449428 Book/CD $14.95

ALTO SAX ► by Jim Odgren and Bill Pierce
50449437 Book/CD $14.95

TENOR SAX ► by Jim Odgren and Bill Pierce
50449431 Book/CD $14.95

TROMBONE ► by Jeff Galindo
50449433 Book/CD $14.95

TRUMPET ► by Tiger Okoshi and Charles Lewis
50449432 Book/CD $14.95

BERKLEE INSTANT SERIES

BASS ► by Danny Morris
50449502 Book/CD $14.95

DRUM SET ► by Ron Savage
50449513 Book/CD $14.95

GUITAR ► by Tomo Fujita
50449522 Book/CD $14.95

KEYBOARD ► by Paul Schmeling and Dave Limina
50449525 Book/CD $14.95

DISTRIBUTED BY
HAL•LEONARD®

IMPROVISATION SERIES

BLUES IMPROVISATION COMPLETE ►
by Jeff Harrington ► Book/CD Packs
50449486 Bb Instruments $19.95
50449488 C Bass Instruments $19.95
50449425 C Treble Instruments $19.95
50449487 Eb Instruments $19.95

A GUIDE TO JAZZ IMPROVISATION
► by John LaPorta ► Book/CD Packs
50449439 C Instruments $16.95
50449441 Bb Instruments $16.95
50449442 Eb Instruments $16.95
50449443 Bass Clef $16.95

MUSIC TECHNOLOGY

ARRANGING IN THE DIGITAL WORLD
► by Corey Allen
50449415 Book/GM disk $19.95

FINALE: AN EASY GUIDE TO MUSIC NOTATION ► by Thomas E. Rudolph and Vincent A. Leonard, Jr.
50449501 Book/CD-ROM $59.95

PRODUCING IN THE HOME STUDIO WITH PRO TOOLS ► by David Franz
50449526 Book/CD-ROM $34.95

RECORDING IN THE DIGITAL WORLD
► by Thomas E. Rudolph and Vincent A. Leonard, Jr.
50449472 Book $29.95

MUSIC BUSINESS

HOW TO GET A JOB IN THE MUSIC & RECORDING INDUSTRY
► by Keith Hatschek
50449505 Book $24.95

THE SELF-PROMOTING MUSICAN
► by Peter Spellman
50449423 Book $24.95

THE MUSICIAN'S INTERNET
► by Peter Spellman
50449527 Book $24.95

REFERENCE

COMPLETE GUIDE TO FILM SCORING
► by Richard Davis
50449417 Book $24.95

THE CONTEMPORARY SINGER
► by Anne Peckham
50449438 Book/CD $24.95

ESSENTIAL EAR TRAINING
► by Steve Prosser
50449421 Book $14.95

MODERN JAZZ VOICINGS ► by Ted Pease and Ken Pullig
50449485 Book/CD $24.95

THE NEW MUSIC THERAPIST'S HANDBOOK, SECOND EDITION
► by Suzanne B. Hanser
50449424 Book $29.95

POP CULTURE

INSIDE THE HITS
► by Wayne Wadhams
50449476 Book $29.95

MASTERS OF MUSIC: CONVERSATIONS WITH BERKLEE GREATS ► by Mark Small and Andrew Taylor
50449422 Book $24.95

SONGWRITING

MELODY IN SONGWRITING
► by Jack Perricone
50449419 Book $19.95

MUSIC NOTATION ► by Mark McGrain
50449399 Book $19.95

SONGWRITING: ESSENTIAL GUIDE TO LYRIC FORM AND STRUCTURE
► by Pat Pattison
50481582 Book $14.95

SONGWRITING: ESSENTIAL GUIDE TO RHYMING ► by Pat Pattison
50481583 Book $14.95